GREAT SPORTING EVENTS

Rugby

Clive Gifford

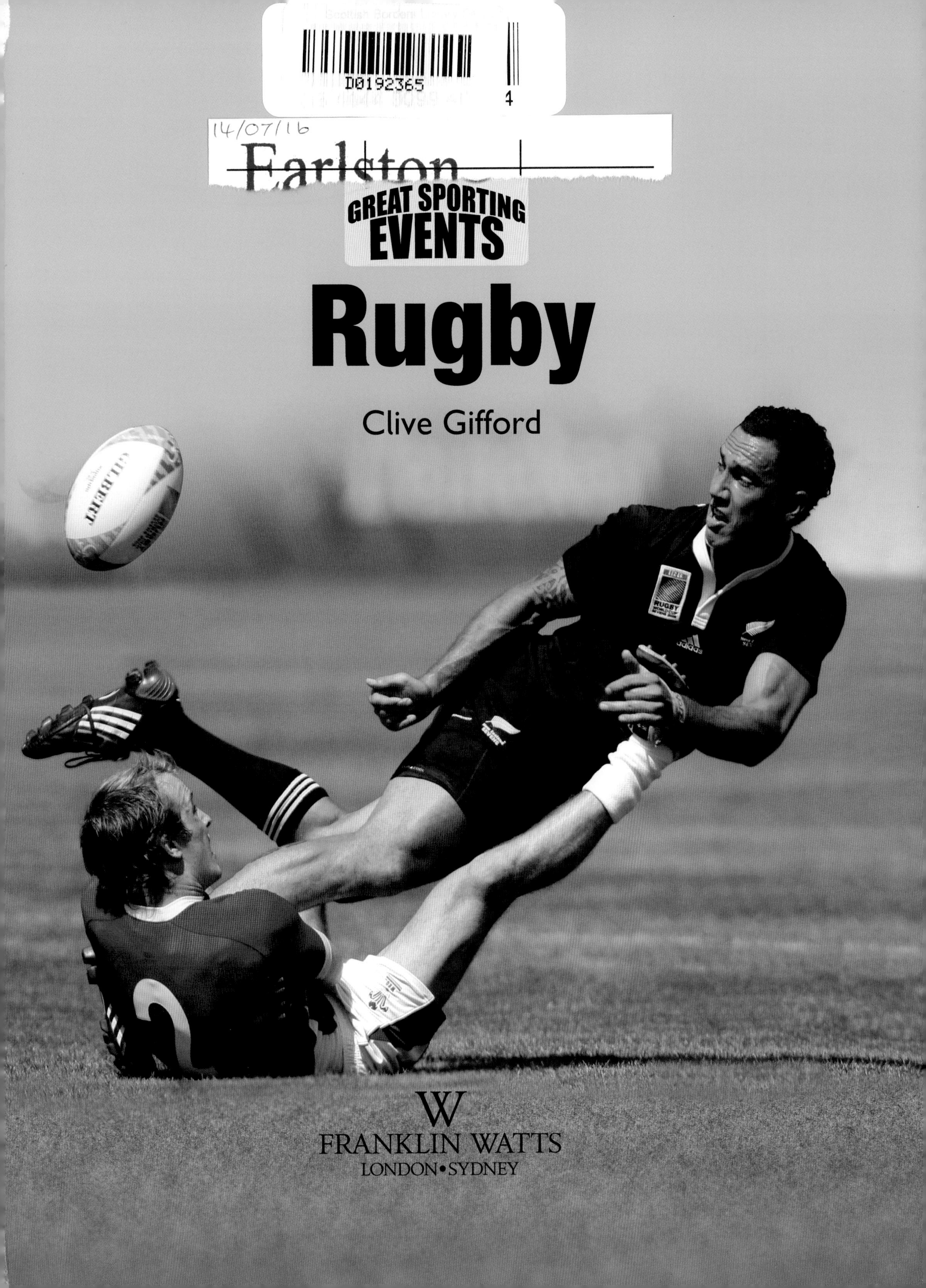

W
FRANKLIN WATTS
LONDON • SYDNEY

Franklin Watts

First published in Great Britain in 2016 by The Watts Publishing Group

Copyright © The Watts Publishing Group, 2016

All rights reserved.

Editors: Katie Dicker & Gerard Cheshire
Art Direction: Rahul Dhiman (Q2AMedia)
Designer: Rohit Juneja, Cheena Yadav (Q2AMedia)
Picture researcher: Nivisha Sinha (Q2AMedia)

Picture credits:
t=top b=bottom c=centre l=left r=right

Front Cover: Ross Setford/NZPA/AP Photo.
Back Cover: Mark J. Terrill/AP Photo, Aijaz Rahi/AP Photo, Dave Thompson/AP Photo, Ross Setford/NZPA/AP Photo, Jay LaPrete/AP Photo, Anja Niedringhaus/AP Photo.
Title Page: Kamran Jebreili/AP Photo.
Imprint Page: Odd Andersen/AP Photo
Insides: Alastair Grant/AP Photo: 4, Mark Baker/AP Photo: 5, Francois Mori/AP Photo: 6, Getty Images for AVIVA: 7, Mark Nolan/Getty Images Sport/Getty Images: 8, Paul Thomas/AP Photo: 9, Tom Hevezi/AP Photo: 10, Claude Paris/AP Photo: 11, Schalk Van Zuydam/AP Photo: 12, David Rowland/NZPA/AP Photo: 13, David Cannon/Getty Images Sport/Getty Images: 14, Peter Morrison/AP Photo: 15, Richard Lewis/AP Photo: 16, Steve Kingsman/Dreamstime: 17, AP Photo: 18, David Rogers/Getty Images: 19, Vincent Yu/AP Photo: 20, Kamran Jebreili/AP Photo: 21, Tertius Pickard/AP Photo: 22, Scott Heppell/AP Photo: 23, Mitch Gunn/Shutterstock: 24, Mark Baker/AP Photo: 25, Adam Davy/Empics Sport/PAI: 26, Tom Hevezi/AP Photo: 27, Jean Catuffe/Getty Images: 26.

Every attempt has been made to clear copyright. Should there be any inadvertent omission, please apply to the publisher for rectification.

ISBN: 978 1 4451 4965 3
Dewey Classification: 796.3'33

Note: At the time of going to press, the statistics in this book were up to date. However, due to the nature of sport, it is possible that some of these may now be out of date.

Printed in China

Franklin Watts
An imprint of
Hachette Children's Group
Part of The Watts Publishing Group
Carmelite House
50 Victoria Embankment
London EC4Y 0DZ

An Hachette UK Company
www.hachette.co.uk

www.franklinwatts.co.uk

FSC
www.fsc.org
MIX
Paper from responsible sources
FSC® C104740

Contents

*Words in **bold** are in the glossary on page 30

Race for the line

Rugby union and rugby league are exciting action sports where teams of players run, pass and kick an oval-shaped ball, beating opponents at high speed to reach the goal line to score a **try**.

Similarities and differences

Both forms of rugby take place on a large grass pitch, with male or female teams competing in a game lasting 80 minutes. There are many differences in rules, however. A rugby union team has 15 players and a rugby league team has 13. There are also no **lineouts** in rugby league.

Tackling defence

The defending team tries to stop the attacking side by **intercepting** passes or tackling the opponent with the ball. In rugby league, a tackled player is allowed to get to his feet and play the ball unopposed. A team gets six tackles before the ball passes to the opposition. In rugby union, there is no set number of tackles and the tackled player must release the ball on the floor once tackled.

In rugby union, a line-out is awarded to a team when the ball has been kicked out of play by a player on the opposing team.

Scoring points

In both rugby union and rugby league, a try is scored when a player puts the ball down on the in-goal, the area beyond the try line at each end of the pitch. A try is worth five points in rugby union and four in rugby league, and is followed by an attempted **conversion** kick through the goalposts for further points. Players can also score points with a penalty kick. This is awarded to a team when a player on the opposing team has committed a **foul** or broken the rules of the game.

Switching sports

Although the rules and **tactics** differ between the two sports, a number of players have switched between them. Two of the most famous were England's Jason Robinson and Australia's Wendell Sailor. Both men were star rugby league players who made the change to rugby union. They played against each other in the 2003 Rugby Union World Cup Final.

England player Jason Robinson (holding ball) played rugby league for eight years before making the switch to rugby union. Here he is playing in a rugby union match.

GREAT SPORTING STATS

	Rugby league	Rugby union
Number of players	13	15
Points for a try	4	5
Points for a drop goal	1	3
Points for a penalty kick	2	3
Points for a conversion kick	2	2

Club rugby union

Most rugby union clubs compete in a competition based on a league format. Teams play matches at their home grounds and away at their opponent's grounds. They gain points for winning or drawing a game.

Foreign imports

A large number of rugby stars play in leagues far away from their home countries. England's James Haskell, for example, has played for English team Wasps, the Ricoh Black Rams in Japan, the Highlanders in New Zealand and the French Top 14 side Stade Français.

Top 14

France's leading club rugby union competition is also one of the oldest, first held in 1892. Starting in August, the teams play 26 games with the top two teams in the league meeting each other for a grand final, usually held in June. After finishing as runners-up ten times, ASM Clermont Auvergne finally triumphed in 2010 beating Perpignan 19-6 in the final.

James Haskell, playing for Stade Français, is tackled by Perpignan's Maxime Mermoz during a Top 14 match.

Pro12

Previously known as the Celtic League and the Magners League, this competition traditionally pits top rugby union sides from Ireland, Wales and Scotland against each other. Fifteen teams began the competition in 2001, but for the 2009/10 season just ten took part – four from Ireland, four from Wales and two from Scotland. Since the 2010/11 season, two Italian teams have also joined the league.

The English Premiership

The English Premiership is the top rugby union league in England and features 12 teams. Since 2000/01, the top four sides at the end of the season contest **semi-finals**, with the winners competing in a single game held at Twickenham Stadium in London for the championship. Leicester Tigers and Wasps have enjoyed remarkable success in recent years, winning ten of the last 15 titles.

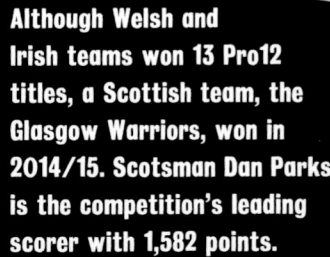

GREAT SPORTING STATS

Although Welsh and Irish teams won 13 Pro12 titles, a Scottish team, the Glasgow Warriors, won in 2014/15. Scotsman Dan Parks is the competition's leading scorer with 1,582 points.

Leicester Tigers' Mathew Tait makes a break during the 2013 English AVIVA Premiership final between Leicester Tigers and Northampton Saints.

Club rugby league

The two biggest club rugby league competitions in the world are based in Australia (the National Rugby League; Est. 1998) and England (the Super League; Est. 1996). Both end with a single game for the championship, called a Grand Final.

National Rugby League (NRL)

Sixteen teams take part in the National Rugby League. Most are based in the Australian state of New South Wales, but there are also three clubs from Queensland and one, the Warriors, based in New Zealand. August and September is the most intense part of the NRL season, with the top eight teams taking part in play-offs, aiming to reach the Grand Final. With three NRL titles, the Brisbane Broncos are the competition's most successful side.

Jason Nightingale scores for the St George Illawarra Dragons against the Sydney Roosters in the 2010 NRL Grand Final. The Dragons won 32–8.

The Super League

The 12 Super League teams are mostly from northern England, but also include the Catalans Dragons from France and formerly the Celtic Crusaders from Wales. They play 23 games – 11 home games, 11 away games and a Magic Weekend game where all the teams play a match at a neutral venue. In 2015, the Magic Weekend took place at St James' Park in Newcastle.

The Grand Final

The eight leading Super League teams play each other once more, and the resulting top four teams enter a semi-final stage leading to the Grand Final. This is held in October at Manchester United FC's Old Trafford stadium, attracting huge crowds. St Helens, the Leeds Rhinos and the Wigan Warriors have reached the Grand Final more often than any other clubs.

World Club Challenge

The winners of the Super League and the NRL champions clash in a single one-off game every year called the World Club Challenge. Recent matches have been exciting, such as the Super League's Leeds Rhinos beating Manly Sea Eagles 26–12 in 2012 (they had lost to Manly 28–20 three years earlier) and NRL's Melbourne Storm beating the Leeds Rhinos 18–14 in 2013.

GREAT SPORTING STATS

England's Danny McGuire was the first player to score 200 tries in Super League and currently holds the record for the most tries (230, for the Leeds Rhinos). The most tries in a single season were scored by Lesley Vainikolo, from Tonga, with 36 tries for the Bradford Bulls in 2004. In the NRL, Australia's Nathan Blacklock was the first player to score 20 or more tries in four consecutive seasons, making him the top try scorer in NRL 1999–2001.

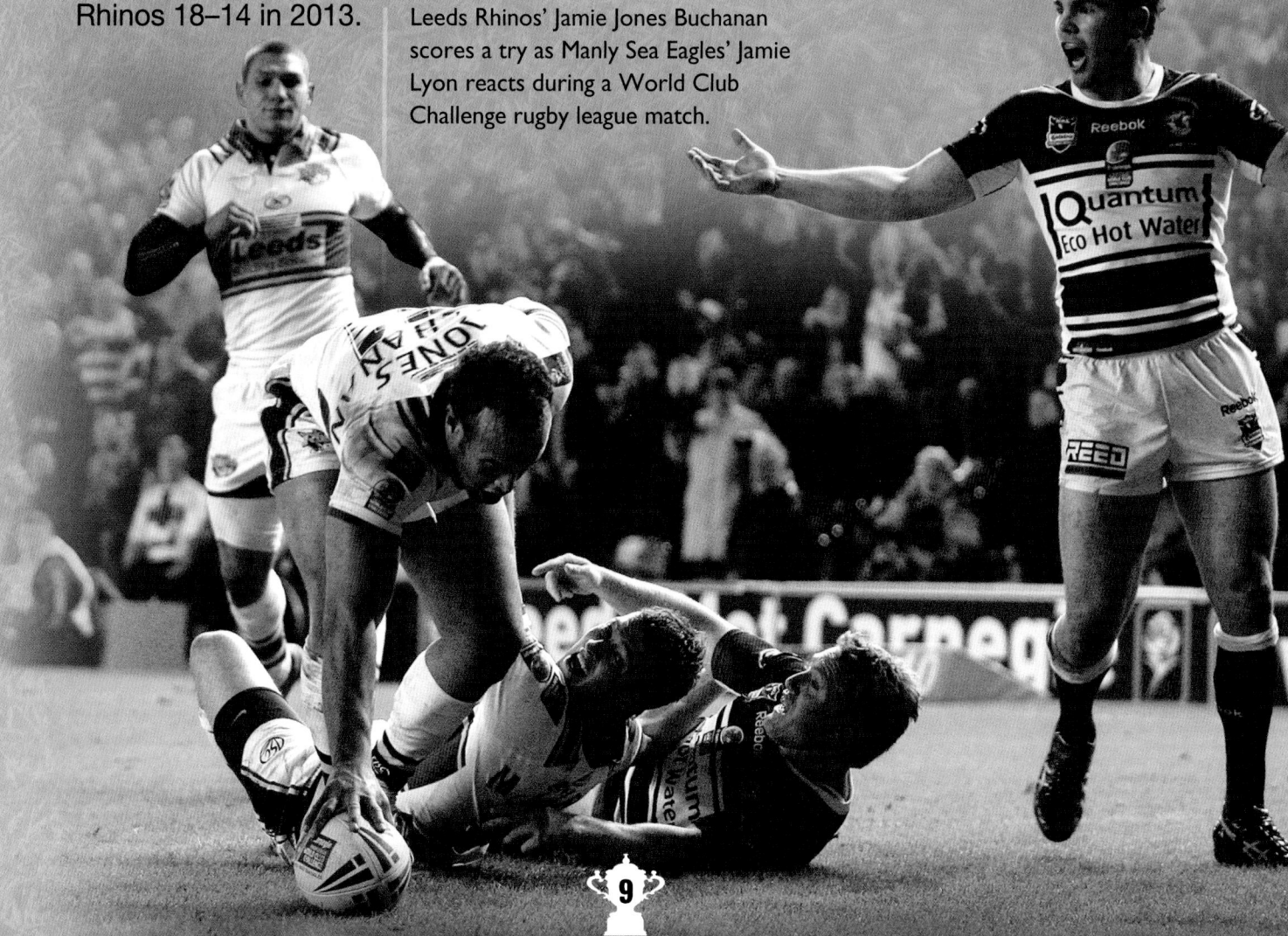

Leeds Rhinos' Jamie Jones Buchanan scores a try as Manly Sea Eagles' Jamie Lyon reacts during a World Club Challenge rugby league match.

The European Rugby Champions Cup

The European Rugby Champions Cup used to be called the Heineken Cup until 2014. The top rugby union club teams from England, France, Ireland, Italy, Scotland and Wales all take part.

Qualification and pools

Teams get to play in the tournament by finishing in the top positions of their country's league the season before. The tournament begins in October with 20 teams, divided into five groups called **pools**, with the pool winners and three best performing runners-up reaching the tournament's **quarter-finals**.

Making the final

The tension mounts as the tournament reaches the semi-finals and final stages. The Leicester Tigers have reached the final five times, but have only won the Cup twice. Toulouse are the most successful side in the competition, with four titles to their name. They also recorded the Cup's biggest ever win, a 108–16 point thrashing of the Welsh team Ebbw Vale in 1998.

Cardiff Blues' Tom James is tackled by Toulouse's Thierry Dusautoir (left) and Jean Bouilhou during a Heineken Cup (now European Rugby Champions Cup) quarter-final match in Cardiff.

Marvellous Munster

The Irish team Munster twice reached the final and lost, before winning the competition in both 2006 and 2008. One of their players, Ronan O'Gara, holds the record for playing in the most European Rugby Champions Cup games – 110 in total. In 2009, Munster lost their semi-final to eventual winners, Leinster, but the 82,208 spectators set a world record at the time for a club rugby union game.

European Rugby Challenge Cup

Top teams who do not qualify for the European Rugby Champions Cup can take part in the European Rugby Challenge Cup. It features 20 teams drawn not only from the British, Irish and French leagues, but also clubs from Italy, Spain, Portugal, Georgia, Romania and Russia.

GREAT SPORTING STATS

Leading points scorers in the European Rugby Champions Cup Cup (1995–2015):
Ronan O'Gara, Ireland: 1,365
Stephen Jones, Wales: 869
Dimitri Yachvili, France: 661
Diego Dominguez, Italy: 645
David Humphreys, Ireland: 564
Neil Jenkins, Wales: 502

The European Rugby Champions Cup's leading points scorer, Ronan O'Gara, strikes a penalty for Munster from close to the **touchline**.

Super Rugby & the Rugby Championship

The leading rugby union-playing nations in the southern hemisphere are Australia, New Zealand and South Africa. They compete as national teams in the Rugby Championship (alongside Argentina), whilst their top club sides take part in a Super Rugby competition.

Super Rugby scoring

The Super Rugby teams are divided into pools and play a series of home-and-away matches in a **round robin** format. Teams are awarded four points for a win, two for a draw and a **bonus point** for teams scoring more than three tries in a game. The winning teams from each pool enter a knockout stage to earn a place in the final.

Competition stars

The Canterbury Crusaders from New Zealand have been the most successful team in the Super Rugby, as champions seven times and runners-up four times. They hold the record for the biggest win (96–19 against the Waratahs) in 2002, and in 2005 scored the most points in a season (541, including 71 tries).

Andries Bekker of the South African Stormers gains **possession** of the ball during a game against the New Zealand Blues in Cape Town, South Africa.

The Rugby Championship

Starting life in 1996 (when it was known as the Tri-Nations), the Rugby Championship pitches Australia, New Zealand, South Africa and newcomers Argentina into a round robin tournament. Teams play each other twice on a home-and-away basis. New Zealand has enjoyed the most success in the competition, winning 13 championships, but games can be close. In the last three matches of the 2009 competition, Australia beat South Africa who then beat New Zealand who, themselves, then beat Australia.

GREAT SPORTING STATS

Rugby Championship Recent Winners	
2007	New Zealand
2008	New Zealand
2009	South Africa
2010	New Zealand
2011	Australia
2012	New Zealand
2013	New Zealand
2014	New Zealand
2015	Australia

South Africa's Victor Matfield lifts the 2009 Tri-Nations trophy (left). By beating New Zealand in the final, South Africa also won the Freedom Cup (right).

The Six Nations

In 1883, an international rugby union competition for the **home nations** of the United Kingdom was first held. France who joined in 1910, turned the competition into the Five Nations, which in 2000 became the Six Nations with the arrival of Italy.

Tournament timings

The tournament begins in February with the first round of games and ends in late March. Since 2002, a Six Nations for the same countries' women's teams (except when Spain replaced Italy between 2002 and 2007) has been held at the same time of the year.

Home and away

The Six Nations is a round robin league competition. Teams play five games in total each season. Two or three are at home and the remainder away. At home, the team plays its games in the same stadium each year. Despite two of the stadia holding over 80,000 fans (London's Twickenham and Paris's Stade de France), demand for tickets is almost as fierce as some of the play on the pitch.

Ireland play Scotland in the 2006 Six Nations tournament. The Irish won the game 15–9 in the last game held at the famous Lansdowne Road stadium in Dublin before it was redeveloped.

Epic rivalries

Scoring is simple, with two points for a win and one for a draw, but the strong, historic rivalries between teams such as England and Scotland mean that matches are often packed with drama and incident. These include Scotland's last-minute 23-20 win over Ireland in 2010, and Ireland's narrow 24-22 defeat of France to secure them the Six Nations title in 2014.

Grand Slams

The dream of any team entering the Six Nations is to complete a Grand Slam: winning all five games and the championship as a result. In 2009, Ireland achieved this for the first time since 1948. Back-to-back grand slams have occurred just five times, the last in 1997 and 1998 by France.

GREAT SPORTING STATS

Two Irish players currently hold impressive records in the Six Nations. Brian O'Driscoll is the leading try scorer, with 26 tries, while Ronan O'Gara is the leading points scorer, with 557 points.

Ireland's Paul O'Connell is tackled by Italy's Gonzalo Garcia during a Six Nations match. O'Connell captained Ireland to a famous Six Nations victory in 2009.

Tours and tests

The rugby world is split between the northern and southern hemispheres, with competitions held at different times of the year. National teams from each hemisphere fly across the planet each year to go on short tours of rival nations.

Summer tours

After the club rugby season has ended in May, British and European national teams often go on tour in early summer. Common destinations are South America to play Argentina and Uruguay, or a daunting visit to the rugby powerhouses of Australia, New Zealand or South Africa which usually takes place in May or June before the Rugby Championship (see page 13) begins.

Dwayne Peel and Ryan Jones, from Wales, take on Jaco van der Westhuyzen, of South Africa, in an international tour match.

Autumn internationals

In October and November most years, the big three southern hemisphere teams, along with teams such as Canada and, sometimes, a Pacific Islanders' side from Fiji, Tonga and Samoa, all tour Europe. They play one or more matches against clubs or regional teams to warm up for big one-off matches against national sides.

Canada (in red) play the mighty Fiji in the 2013 Pacific Nations Cup.

Tough test

For the host nations of Britain, Ireland and France, the autumn internationals are a tough test. In 2014, for example, England faced New Zealand, South Africa, Samoa and Australia in successive weekends. Victories can be rare but notable for the home teams, such as Ireland's impressive wins over South Africa and Australia in 2014.

The Pacific Nations Cup

Founded in 2006, the Pacific Nations Cup is held between six nations bordering the Pacific Ocean (Fiji, Japan, Samoa, Tonga, Canada and the United States). The tournament was set up to provide a series of competitive matches to strengthen these rugby nations. Fiji won their third title in a row in 2015.

GREAT SPORTING STATS

In 2014, Wales's 12-6 defeat of South Africa in the autumn internationals was something to celebrate. It was only the second time Wales had beaten South Africa in over a hundred years (the first being in 1999).

The British and Irish Lions

The British and Irish Lions is the most famous rugby touring side of all. Players and coaches take on the challenge of a trip once every four years to one of the three biggest rugby-playing nations in the southern hemisphere.

Picking the team

The first tour made by an official Lions team was to South Africa in 1910, although a combined Irish and British team had visited Australia in 1888. Today, a selection panel sits with the head coach and picks players from Ireland, England, Scotland and Wales to form a squad of around 40 players. To be picked to go on a Lions tour is a major honour.

On tour

The Lions have just a few short weeks to train together and get to know their new team-mates before they go on tour. The tour consists of a number of matches against regional teams, and three test matches against the home side's national team, which in 2013 was Australia.

British Lions' scrum-half Dickie Jeeps looks to make a pass during the third Test of the 1955 Lions tour of South Africa.

Winger George North of the British & Irish Lions is tackled by James O'Connor of the Australian Wallabies during a 2013 Test in Sydney, Australia.

Dirt trackers

As the tour progresses, many of the players learn that they will not be selected for the first Test. These '**dirt trackers**' will still have to perform in the regional games and support their team-mates, but may get a chance later in the tour. In 2009, Welsh player Shane Williams wasn't selected for the first two Tests, but when he appeared in the third, he scored two tries.

GREAT SPORTING STATS

Ireland's Willie John McBride has played the most Tests for the Lions – 17 in total. The three leading Lions points scorers have all played six Tests – England's Jonny Wilkinson (67 points), Scotland's Gavin Hastings (66 points) and Wales's Stephen Jones (53 points).

Future secured

Doubts existed over the Lions' future after a 2–1 defeat against Australia in 2001 and a disastrous 3–0 series loss in New Zealand in 2005. These were erased by an incredibly exciting series against South Africa in 2009, where the Lions lost narrowly 2–1, but beat South Africa in the final Test in thrilling style, 28–9. Then in 2013, the Lions beat Australia 2-1.

International rugby sevens

Rugby sevens is an exciting, attacking version of rugby union played on a full-sized pitch, but with just seven players a side. Games are short and incredibly direct with three-man **scrums** and the emphasis on attacking play.

Points scoring

Tries, penalties and conversions are worth the same in sevens as they are in regular rugby union, although conversions have to be taken as a **drop kick**. Despite games only lasting 14 minutes, with one minute break between halves, scoring can be high. In a 2010 Hong Kong Sevens semi-final, New Zealand beat Fiji 33–28.

One of the greatest ever rugby sevens' players, Fiji's Waisale Serevi, runs for a last try against New Zealand in the Hong Kong Sevens.

Hong Kong Sevens

Teams usually play a series of games in a day or weekend tournament. Amongst the most famous of all tournaments is the Hong Kong Sevens, held at the end of March every year since 1976. There's a festive atmosphere in the crowd and outrageous attacking play on the pitch. This often comes from Pacific island teams such as Fiji who have won the tournament 15 times, and Samoa who won for the third time in 2010.

World Rugby Sevens Series

This is a series of tournaments run by World Rugby. The higher a team finishes at a tournament, the more points it earns. The team with the most points in a series is the winner. New Zealand has won an impressive 12 titles in 16 years (2000-2015).

Rugby World Cup Sevens

Held every four years (since 1993 for men and 2009 for women), this is the ultimate sevens tournament. England, New Zealand and Fiji have all won the men's World Cup, whilst Wales became surprise champions in 2009. In the same year, Australia won the first women's tournament.

New Zealand's Zar Lawrence (right) passes the ball while being tackled by Wales's Lee Williams during the semi-finals of the Rugby World Cup Sevens in Dubai, UAE, in 2009.

GREAT SPORTING STATS

Top World Rugby Sevens Series points scorers:
Ben Gollings (England) 2,652
Tomasi Cama (New Zealand) 2,026
Colin Gregor (Scotland) 1,345
Uale Mai (Samoa) 1,320
Waisale Serevi (Fiji) 1,310

International rugby league

The Rugby League World Cup was first held in 1954 and is much older than the rugby union version (see pages 24–25). Over the years, the format has changed, but only three teams – Australia, Great Britain and New Zealand – have ever won it.

Expanding numbers

In 1995, the tournament was expanded from five to ten teams, allowing sides such as Samoa, Fiji, South Africa and Tonga to enter. Team numbers grew to 16 in 2000 but dropped back to ten teams in 2008. Since 2013, the tournament has expanded back to 14 teams and is now expected to take place every four years.

New Zealand's Sam Perrett clashes with Australia's Cameron Smith (right) during the Rugby League World Cup Final in Brisbane, Australia, 2008.

Fabulous finals

Amongst the greatest finals were Australia's nail-biting 13–12 win over Great Britain in 1977, and the 2008 final in which firm favourites, Australia, were beaten 34–20 by New Zealand. Both team captains, Australia's Darren Lockyer and New Zealand's Nathan Cayless, were the only remaining players from the previous World Cup Final back in 2000.

Tri-Nations and Four Nations

A desire for more regular international rugby league saw the Tri-Nations series between Australia, Great Britain and New Zealand kick off in 1999. The teams played each other once (from 2004, twice) and then the top two teams played a final.

In 2009, the competition was replaced by a Four Nations series. The additional team is either the winner of the Rugby League European Cup (competed for by the top European teams, excluding England), or the winner of the Pacific Rugby League International, depending on whether the competition is being played in the northern or southern hemisphere.

England's Kyle Eastmond is halted by New Zealand's Issac Luke (right) and Kieran Foran (left) during a Four Nations rugby league match.

The Rugby World Cup

The Rugby Union World Cup began in 1987 and is held every four years. Although around 100 teams attempt to qualify, just 20 take part in the tournament. All are hoping to get their hands on the famous Webb Ellis trophy.

New Zealand perform their famous haka dance at the start of a 2015 Rugby Union World Cup group match against Namibia.

Hosting nations

World Cup hosts are selected many years ahead to give the countries time to upgrade their facilities. For the 1999 World Cup, for example, Wales built the magnificent Millennium Stadium in Cardiff. Some tournaments are co-hosted, such as in 2007, when France were the main hosts but some games were held in Scotland and Wales. The next tournament will be held in Japan in 2019.

Massive interest

Only 17,768 people turned up to watch France beat Australia in a pulsating semi-final at the first World Cup. Since that time, the tournament has boomed in popularity. Over 2.4 million people went to see the 48 games played at the 2015 tournament in England, with 80,125 spectators watching the final.

Southern dominance

All the World Cups so far have been won by South Africa, New Zealand or Australia, with the exception of England's 2003 victory, thanks to Jonny Wilkinson's last-minute drop goal. Many other sides have had their turn in the spotlight, however. At the 2015 tournament, Scotland nearly beat Australia in a thrilling quarter-finals (they lost 35-34). Their stunning play saw them come very close to reaching the semi-finals for the first time since 1991. Australia then went on to the final, where they lost to New Zealand (34-17). For the second tournament in a row, Argentina also made it to the semi-finals, beating Ireland along the way.

England's Jonny Wilkinson converts another penalty during the Rugby World Cup semi-final against France in 2003.

GREAT SPORTING STATS

Jonny Wilkinson's 277 points for England in four World Cups are the most scored by a player, whilst New Zealand's Grant Fox scored the most in one World Cup with 126 points in 1987. The record try scorer was New Zealand's Jonah Lomu with 15 tries.

Women's rugby

Women's rugby union and rugby league is booming. Teams play under the same rules and on the same size pitches as men, in a variety of competitions for club teams and national sides.

Club rugby league

Australia, New Zealand and England are home to most of the world's women's rugby league clubs. In Australia, competitions are mostly run at state level. The best players from the Australian states of Queensland and New South Wales play each other in the State of Origin series. In England, around 35 teams compete in the women's rugby league. The Featherstone Rovers were the most successful side in 2015.

International rugby league

Four nations – Australia, New Zealand, England and France – compete in rugby league test matches against each other. In 2005 and 2008, they joined other nations (such as Tonga, Russia, Samoa and the Pacific Islands) to form an eight-team Women's Rugby League World Cup. In 2013, the original four teams took part with Australia winning the Cup. The tournament is now held once every four years.

New Zealand's captain Laura Mariu lines up the ball for a conversion kick in the final of the 2000 Rugby League World Cup against Britain & Ireland.

Club rugby union

Increasingly large numbers of women's rugby union clubs take part in leading cup and league competitions, such as the National Women's Championship in Australia, the Women's All Ireland League and the SWRU Premier League in Scotland. In England, the leading women's teams such as Richmond Women and Saracens Women compete in a Premiership league.

Women's Rugby Union World Cup

First held in 1991, when the winners were the USA, this competition features 12 teams from all over the world. The 2014 tournament in France included teams from Samoa, Canada and Kazakhstan, as well as South Africa, Australia, New Zealand, England and Wales. England won the tournament for the first time since 1994.

GREAT SPORTING STATS

Selica Winiata and Shakira Baker of New Zealand were leading try scorers at the 2014 Women's Rugby Union World Cup with six tries each. England's Emily Scarratt finished as the top points scorer with 70 points.

England celebrate winning the 2014 Women's Rugby Union World Cup.

WOMEN'S
RUGBY WORLD CUP
2014

Timeline and winner tables

1871 The first international rugby match between teams from Scotland and England.

1877 A rule change cuts down the number of players in a team from 20 to 15.

1886 The International Rugby Board (IRB) is formed, to run world rugby.

1895 A breakaway group of rugby clubs form the Northern Rugby League.

1896 The first Rugby League Challenge Cup is held.

1910 France joins the Home Nations to form the Five Nations competition.

1924 The last appearance of rugby union at the Olympics.

1954 The Rugby League World Cup is formed.

1971 The number of points for a rugby union try increases from three to four.

1976 The Hong Kong Sevens competition is held for the first time.

1980 The first State of Origin match occurs, between Queensland and New South Wales.

1982 The first official women's international rugby union match is played between the Netherlands and France.

1983 The number of points for a rugby league try increases from three to four.

1987 The New Zealand All Blacks win the Rugby World Cup, beating France in the final.

1991 The first Women's Rugby Union World Cup is hosted in Wales.

1992 The number of points for a rugby union try increases from four to five points.

1993 The first Rugby Sevens World Cup is held at Murrayfield, in Edinburgh.

1995 IRB declares rugby union to be an open sport, allowing full professionalism for the first time.

1996 The Tri-Nations Rugby Union series starts between Australia, New Zealand and South Africa.

1996 Rugby League's Super League begins.

1998 The National Rugby League competition starts in Australia.

2000 The Five Nations becomes the Six Nations when Italy joins.

2003 England win their first ever Rugby Union World Cup, beating Australia.

2015 The Rugby World Cup is held in England.

2016 Rugby sevens is included as a medal sport at the Olympics for the first time.

The British Lions play South Africa during their four-match series in 1955.

Winner tables

Men's Rugby Union World Cup

Year	Winners	Runners-up
1995	South Africa	New Zealand
1999	Australia	France
2003	England	Australia
2007	South Africa	England
2011	New Zealand	France
2015	New Zealand	Australia

Women's Rugby Union World Cup

Year	Winners	Runners-up
1994	England	USA
1998	New Zealand	USA
2002	New Zealand	England
2006	New Zealand	England
2010	New Zealand	England
2014	England	Canada

Rugby World Cup Sevens (Men's)

Year	Winners	Runners-up
1997	Fiji	South Africa
2001	New Zealand	Australia
2005	Fiji	New Zealand
2009	Wales	Argentina
2013	New Zealand	England

Rugby League World Cup (Men's)

Year	Winners	Runners-up
1957	Australia	Great Britain
1960	Great Britain	Australia
1968	Australia	France
1970	Australia	Great Britain
1972	Great Britain	Australia
1975	Australia	England
1977	Australia	Great Britain
1985–88	Australia	New Zealand
1989–92	Australia	Great Britain
1995	Australia	England
2000	Australia	New Zealand
2008	New Zealand	Australia
2013	Australia	New Zealand

Glossary and further info

Bonus points   A system used in some league competitions of awarding extra points to teams for close games or for scoring many tries.

Conversion   A kick awarded after a try, which, if it travels between the goal posts, is worth two points.

Dirt trackers   A slang term given to players in a touring squad who tend only to play in the less important matches of a tour.

Drop goal   A points-scoring move where the ball is kicked out of the hand between the goalposts.

Drop kick   A kick made from the hands with the ball dropped down and struck just before it reaches the ground.

Foul   A breaking of the rules of a game of rugby such as tackling an opponent in a dangerous manner.

Home nations   The countries that make up the United Kingdom: England, Scotland, Wales and Northern Ireland.

Intercepting   When a member of the defending team gathers the ball during a pass made by the opposing team.

Lineout   A way of restarting play in rugby union when the ball has left the side of the pitch. The ball is thrown into the middle of rows of players from each team.

Pools   Small groups of teams in some rugby competitions who all play each other, with one or more teams qualifying from the pool to play in the next round of the tournament.

Possession   When a player or team has the ball under control.

Quarter-final   The four games played with the four winners taking part in the semi-final of a competition.

Round robin   A type of competition format where each team plays all the other teams in their group.

Scrum   A way of restarting play which involves eight players a side in rugby union and six players per side in rugby league.

Semi-final   The two games played with the two winners taking part in the final of a competition.

Tactics   Styles of play and moves which a team and a coach work on to try to beat the opposing team.

Touchline   The lines marking the side edges of the pitch.

Try   Getting the ball placed down under control in the in-goal area of the pitch which is worth five points in rugby union and four in rugby league.

Wingers   Fast, attacking players in both rugby league and rugby union who have to defend but aim to create or score tries.

World Rugby   The organisation that runs international rugby union.

Websites

http://www.worldrugby.org
The official website of World Rugby, the organisation that runs international rugby union including the World Cup.

http://www.rugbyworldcup.com
The 2015 Rugby World Cup website with details of qualifying, fixtures and statistics from all the past competitions.

http://www.rbs6nations.com/en/home.php
The official website of the Six Nations competition.

http://www.epcrugby.com/home.php
A website about European club rugby with lots of information and news on the European Rugby Champions Cup.

http://www.rugby.com.au
The official website of Australian rugby union offers up to the minute coverage of both the Australian national rugby union team, the Rugby Championship and all the Super Rugby action.

http://www.superxv.com
The official website of the Super Rugby contest gives all the details of the current tournament as well as information on previous competitions.

http://www.scrumqueens.com
An information-packed website for women's international rugby union with news of tournaments from all around the world.

http://www.planetrugby.com
Learn more about international rugby union at this website with news and competitions searchable by country.

http://www.espn.co.uk/rugby
A website packed with news, views, photos, results and statistics on rugby union all over the planet.

http://www.rugbysevens.co.uk
A useful website for newcomers to rugby sevens with rules and playing guides as well as details of leading sevens tournaments in Britain and abroad.

http://www.rugbyleagueplanet.com
Learn more about international rugby league at this website with facts, news and profiles from all the main rugby league-playing nations.

http://www.therfl.co.uk/index.php
The Rugby Football League website has a handy guide to the game as well as details of all levels of rugby league competition.

Further reading

Total Rugby Union – Paul Morgan (A&C Black Publishers Ltd, 2008)
A good starting guide to the sport and its leading players.

Know Your Sport: Rugby – Clive Gifford (Franklin Watts, 2010/2012)
Find out about rugby tactics and techniques and some of the world's biggest tournaments.

Index